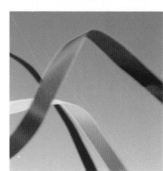

MILWAUKEE

photography by todd dacquisto

PRAIRIE OAK PRESS

A subsidiary of Trails Media Group, Inc.
Black Earth, Wisconsin

Library of Congress Catalog Card Number: 2002105563
ISBN: 1-931599-14-9

Photography by Todd Dacquisto
Design and Photo Editing by Kathie Campbell

Printed in China by Four Colour Imports, Ltd.

06 05 04 03 02   6 5 4 3 2 1

Prairie Oak Press, a subsidiary of Trails Media Group, Inc.
P.O. Box 317 • Black Earth, WI 53515
(800) 236-8088 • e-mail: books@wistrails.com
www.trailsbooks.com

To Lisa, Talia & Sienna
Love ∞

O'Donnell Park sculpture, *Pledge Allegiance* by Glenna Goodacre

Five-by-eight-foot stained glass installed in 1931 in Milwaukee's City Hall

WE KNOW WHAT MOST babies' first words are, but I'm a longtime Milwaukeean and I like to think that my first word was Kinnickinnic, or maybe Teutonia, or Vilet.

As a local journalist, I know this city well, but street photographers know Milwaukee much better. And Todd Daquisto is a street and avenue and parkway and terrace and mall and bridge and byway and backstage and lake and festival and parade and people photographer. Milwaukee is his city and some of his photographs in this book surprise me because I hadn't noticed these things while I've been out and about for the last 60 years.

Todd was born in the Milwaukee area, has lived most of his life here, and says that English is his second language. Images are his first and he sure shows that here.

He seems to see everything through a viewfinder, although I hope he doesn't drive that way. You know how you feel when you walk into a strange room and look for some place to lean, or someone who'll talk to you? Todd walks into a strange room and his first thought is how to light it. His second thought is how to frame it. His heart doesn't beat, it clicks.

Todd is a perfectionist and if he were hired to photograph the last day of the world, he'd probably ask to re-shoot it after it was over.

I met Todd in the early '80s, when he was the lead photographer for a project for the Department of City Development in Milwaukee. Todd needed an aging, baggy-eyed, underweight, graying, stumbling, bumbling journalist, and that's how he found me to shoot in the city room of the old *Milwaukee Sentinal.*

I never understood why he got me involved, but the project was called "Spirit of Milwaukee." And Todd's never been far from photographing that spirit, which is what his book and his life are about.

You won't find babushkas in his book, or Polish or German script. That is the city's past and Todd's focus is the now and the coming. His pictures show the vitality and the shine. And they show the wonder, as the city transforms today into tomorrow, building the foundation for the rest of this century, which he's determined to light and frame and photograph until the film runs out.

"This book is not a snapshot of the city," Todd said. "It's not a drive-by view of Milwaukee. It's on foot. You look up and you look down."

He looked down, way down, as he photographed from a swing that was 30-odd floors above the ground, while a couple of high wire workers did some window caulking. He scampered to the top of the Domes in Mitchell Park. The Coast Guard dropped him off on the breakwater, just him and his cameras and his imagination and the water, and, thank god, they remembered to pick him up. The Milwaukee County Sheriff's Department got him a perch on the congested High Rise Bridge downtown and he took the most dramatic photograph of Miller Park you've ever seen.

He also looked up, way up, as he lay on the floor at the Central Library so he could photograph a gem unseen by most of us—the ceiling, which is a spectacular work of art, and he produced a photograph that was worthy of it.

Todd crawled and he scaled, trying to get pictures that show the city who, what and why it is. He walked, charged, and sauntered through the city's seasons, snapping winter's hills of salt, spring's chestnut groves downtown, summer's blaze orange skies, and fall's dripping hues. He aimed at church tiles and fish fries. He looked for excitement in color, and in concrete, and recorded it all with great warmth.

Todd's pictures show deep feeling, which is the most important part of his transparencies.

Several years ago, Todd signed a contract to do this book, but he postponed the work when his wife, Lisa, was seriously ill with a brain tumor. She died in 2000 and Todd is raising their two lovely daughters, Talia and Sienna, whom he photographed for this book.

During Lisa's illness, a group of wonderful photographers, designers and art directors gave Lisa and Todd and their children great support and staged a charitable auction. Todd will never forget these beautiful people who helped his family.

He loves this city. And his photographs show it.

Bill Janz, 2002
Reporter and columnist for the Milwaukee Sentinel
and the Milwaukee Journal Sentinel *for 40 years.*

MILWAUKEE
spring

Snowfall on spring flowers along the lakefront

Kids maple sugaring at Schlitz Audubon Center

Runner along breakwater at dawn
The Milwaukee Art Museum Calatrava-designed addition (page 1)

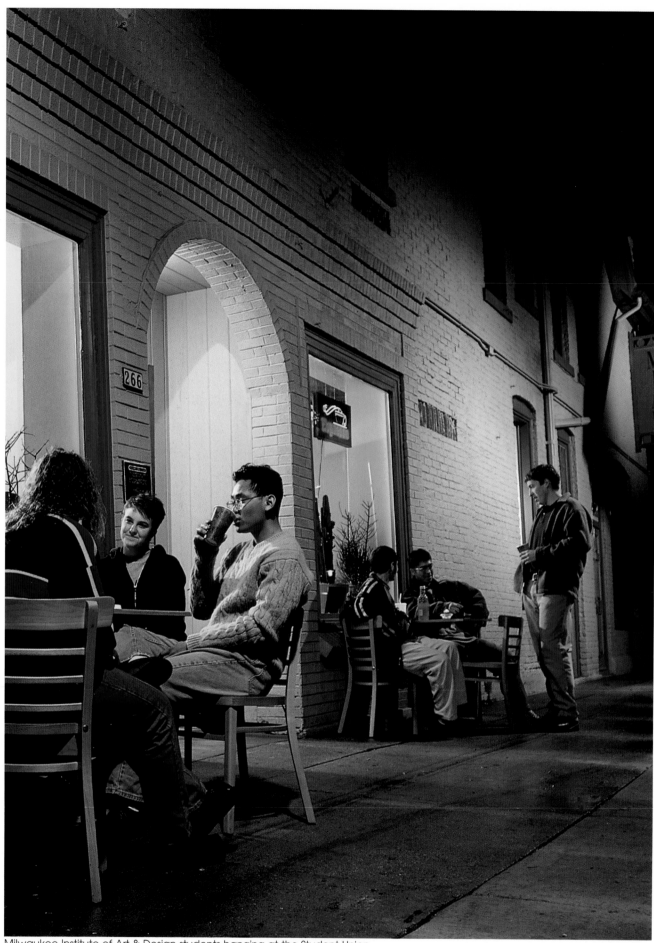

Milwaukee Institute of Art & Design students hanging at the Student Union

Flowering trees in Chestnut Grove at the Marcus Center for the Performing Arts

McKinley Marina taken from the breakwater looking southwest

The Oriental Theater lobby with its motif of the East Indies, built in 1927

Flowering trees along Old World Third Street

Building reflections in the Firstar Building

Aboard the *Denis Sullivan,* a schooner built in Milwaukee to educate about freshwater resources and maritime heritage

Milwaukee Art Museum Calatrava-designed addition interior

Marquette University Cudahy Building between classes

The Cherry Street bridge control tower

Calatrava-designed addition to the Milwaukee Art Museum

Sun glistening off Milwaukee Center Building

Sandblasting oil stacks in the Port of Milwaukee

Trinity Evangelical Lutheran Church with MATC in the foreground

Painted wall near Golda Meir School

Typical older neighborhood downtown

Humphrey Scottish Rites Building detail (left) and Buffalo Building detail (right)

Hair Do by Bobby Joe Scribner, part of RiverWalk's RiverSculpture rotating sculptures

Looking east along Wisconsin Avenue

Gondola along the RiverWalk

Terrace at O'Donnell Park along the Lakefront

440th Airlift Wing at General Mitchell Field

The Oriental Theater Kimball pipe organ, built in 1927

Ship and tugboat in the Milwaukee Harbor

McKinley Marina at dawn

Tripoli Shrine Temple Dome, the first Shrine Temple in Wisconsin, built in 1885

Milwaukee County Library dome interior

St Josephat Basilica Dome interior

St Josephat Basilica Dome, built in 1901

MILWAUKEE
summer

Employee inspection of the Wisconsin Gas Company Flame, which changes color according to the weather

Harley Davidson's 95th Anniversary held in Milwaukee

West Towne Farmers' Market held on Wednesdays at Zeidler Union Square Park
Miller Park (pages 26-27)

City Hall clock tower through Plaza East Towers

Young face-painted girl celebrating July 4th by eating a bombpop

International Cycling Classic, since 1969, featuring racers from 22 countries

North Avenue Tower with the UW-Milwaukee cross-country team in training

Puelicher Butterfly Wing at Milwaukee Public Museum

Greater Milwaukee Open at
Brown Deer Golf Course

Along the RiverWalk at The Harp

35

Summerfest clown in skytram

Miller Inn™ after a tour of Miller Brewing Company

Since 1870, George Watts & Son has specialized in fine china, crystal and gifts

Milwaukee Institute of Art and Design (MIAD) graduate in front of an installation piece on Gallery Night in the Third Ward

Have a Nice Day Cafe nightclub patrons surround employee

Southeast Wisconsin Vietnam Veteran's Memorial in Veteran's Park, made of Wausau Red Granite, dedicated in 1991

Up and Under live jazz club for over 25 years, located on the east side

The annual Milwaukee Bucks Hoop It up 3 on 3 basketball tournament held downtown

Lakefront Festival of Arts, one of the country's finest juried art festivals

Two friends enjoying a latte at Alterra Roastery (roasting since 1993) on Milwaukee's East side

Suits of armor from Augsburg, Germany, dating from 1560 at Mader's Restaurant

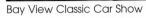

Bay View Classic Car Show

Trigon by Allen Ditson alongside Chestnut Grove at the Marcus Center for the Performing Arts

Fourth of July Fireworks

Asian Moon Festival young perfomers waiting to go on stage

Rainbow Summer, free summer-long concerts on the RiverWalk at Peck Pavilion

Interacting with the weather station at Discovery World Museum

America's largest Polish Festival held at Maier Festival Park

Milwaukee Mile Nascar Race held at State Fair Park

Rainbow Summer at the Marcus Center for Performing Arts' Peck Pavilion

View of the Third Ward from the south

Irishfest, the world's largest celebration of Irish culture and music

Kite Fly-in at Veteran's Park

Polish Fest

Festa Italiana, America's largest Italian cultural event

MILWAUKEE
autumn

Ko-Thi, an original dance company for 30 years in Milwaukee

Milwaukee Harbor at sunrise

Eisner Museum's Radio Studio, the country's only museum of Advertising and Design
Bradley Sculpture Garden (pages 58-59)

Young girl hanging from a branch at Boerner Botanical Gardens

Milwaukee Symphony Orchestra performing at the Marcus Center for the Performing Arts

Milwaukee Bucks game at Bradley Center

Al's Run annual benefit for cancer research

Fritsche School gym class in Humboldt Park

Hurling Club match

Milwaukee Bucks basketball at Bradley Center

Floating Sculpture No. 3 by Marta Pan, 1972, the pond at Bradley Sculpture Gardens

Maintenance of the City Hall bell, *Solomon Juneau*

Mitchell Park Horticultural Conservatory/The Domes, the only horticulture structure of its kind in the world

Forty-horse hitch pulling the Two Hemispheres Band Wagon in the Great Circus Parade

Woman with puppet at the International Holiday Folk Fair

Overlook from the Observation Tower at Schlitz Audubon Center

Handsome Barber Shop, purchased by Richard Moore in 1947, now run by two sons and two grandsons

Milwaukee Brewers' pregame tailgaters

Fly fishing on the Milwaukee River

House near the South Shore Yacht Club

Pabst Theater, built in 1895, restored in 1976, national historic landmark

Newborn in St. Joseph's Regional Medical Center, baby hospital of Milwaukee

Students rehearsing jazz at Milwaukee High School of the Arts

Students at Milwaukee Sign Language School

Students at Milwaukee French Immersion School

Aerial of lighthouse in Lake Park

St. Sava Serbian Orthodox Cathedral

The Lovers, a bronze statue by Lindsay Daen, 1964, Bradley Sculpture Garden

MILWAUKEE
winter

Olympic hopeful training at Pettit Center

Sledding down St. Mary's Hill along the lakefront (above and top)
Snow Angel on a hillside along the lakefront (pages 86-87)

Along the lakefront lower part of Lake Park

Cross-country skier north of Bradford Beach on lakefront

Pabst Mansion during the holiday season, a national historic landmark built in 1895

Iron gates leading to gardens at Villa Terrace

Sledding down St. Mary's Hill and snowshoeing along Lake Michigan in Schlitz Audubon Nature Center

Christmas in the Ward

Poinsettias at Milwaukee County Greenhouse

Fish fry at American Serb Hall

Polar Bear Club New Year's Day swim in Lake Michigan

Winter kayaking on Milwaukee River

International Snow Sculpture Competition

Snow-laden trees along the RiverWalk

acknowledgements

THE BEST PART OF MY JOB as a photographer is having the opportunity to meet an incredibly diverse mix of people. The interactions with people from all walks of life and from all corners of the world are what make my life experience rich. One of the best things about Milwaukee is the people who call it home. There were many Milwaukeeans who went above and beyond the call of duty in helping me produce the images in this book and I thank each and every one of them.

On many of the photo adventures, Pat Jazweicki (a Milwaukee-based photographer and assistant) provided help. I am grateful for his interest in this project. Thanks to Lt. Sundland of the U.S. Coast guard and his crew for providing taxi service for a unique perspective of the fireworks and to Sheriff Lev Baldwin for his assistance in obtaining a dramatic view of Miller Park. To the Milwaukee Police Department, District 1, Lt. Alexander for trying to accommodate all of my strange requests and for never saying no. Thanks to Megan McCarthy at Wisconsin Gas Company for a close-up look at the flame atop that beautiful building. Thanks to the Ko-Thi Dance Troupe for their contribution. To Clark Hillary of the Milwaukee Bucks, Dave Herrell of the Bradley Center, Laura Handles of the Pettit Center, Lori Dealey from Wisconsin's Flagship *Denis Sullivan*, the Board of Directors of Bradley Sculpture Garden, Vicki Reddin of the Milwaukee Art Museum and from the Milwaukee County Zoo—Jennifer Diliberti and Tracey Dolphin—thanks for accommodating my photo requests. Thanks to Becky Lang, Stephan Smith, Stephen Weinstein, Susan Loris, John Dahlman, Dawn Day Hourigan, Dave Austin, Dan Blackman, The Moore family, everyone at Alterra, William Janz and Mr. Durdka. And for those who helped me in one way or another and are not mentioned here, thanks.

Thanks to Madison-based photographer Zane Williams for making the connection and getting me involved in this project. You are and always have been a source of inspiration for me.

This Milwaukee book project has taught me so much about life. It has reaffirmed my belief in the human spirit. The patience and confidence that Trails Media Group offered me was not only needed, but also greatly appreciated. I am forever grateful to them for believing in me and allowing me to adjust the timeline to accommodate the stress and challenges that Cancer presented. Thanks to my mom Dorothy, Anna Lisa, family, friends and neighbors who covered for me when the sun shined and my cameras beckoned. And to Talia and Sienna who make everything in life worthwhile and are the center of my universe. But most of all, thanks to Lisa, who added so much to my world and showed me how to balance all of life's demands, never losing sight of what's important. May her spirit soar.

todd dacquisto

AFTER GRADUATING FROM the UW-Madison Business School Todd Dacquisto tried to fit into the "suit and tie" corporate world. But after eight months, Todd decided to heed the call of his right brain and started his own photography business. As a self taught photographer, Todd was fortunate to spend time with some of his photography idols who continue to influence his work including Jay Maisel, Chris Callis, and Gregory Heisler. Todd's specialty is photographing people on location. He has traveled all over the world creating images for advertising, corporate reports, brochures, and magazines.